Native Americans

The Nature Company Discoveries Library published by Time-Life Books

Conceived and produced by
Weldon Owen Pty Limited
43 Victoria Street, McMahons Point,
NSW, 2060, Australia
A member of the
Weldon Owen Group of Companies
Sydney • San Francisco
Copyright © 1995 US Weldon Owen Inc.
Copyright © 1995 Weldon Owen Pty Limited
Reprinted 1996 (four times), 1997

THE NATURE COMPANY
Priscilla Wrubel, Ed Strobin, Steve Manning,
Georganne Papac, Tracy Fortini

TIME-LIFE BOOKS
Time-Life Books is a division of Time Life Inc.
Time-Life is a trademark of Time Warner Inc.
U.S.A.

Time-Life Custom Publishing
Vice President and Publisher: Terry Newell
Director of New Product Development:
Quentin McAndrew
Managing Editor: Donia Ann Steele
Director of Sales: Neil Levin
Director of Financial Operations: J. Brian Birky

WELDON OWEN Pty Limited
Chairman: Kevin Weldon
President: John Owen
Publisher: Sheena Coupe
Managing Editor: Rosemary McDonald
Text Editor: Claire Craig
Educational Consultants: Richard L. Needham,
Deborah A. Powell
Art Director: Sue Burk
Designers: Juliet Cohen, Gary Fletcher,
Kylie Mulquin
Assistant Designer: Janet Marando
Picture Research Coordinator: Esther Beaton
Picture Research: Amanda Parsonage,
Lorann Pendleton, Fay Torres-Yap

Production Manager: Caroline Webber
Production Assistant: Kylie Lawson
Vice President, International Sales:
Stuart Laurence
Coeditions Director: Derek Barton

Text: Judith Simpson

Illustrators: Helen Halliday; Adam Hook/
Bernard Thornton Artists, UK; Richard Hook/
Bernard Thornton Artists, UK; Keith Howland;
Janet Jones; David Kirshner; Mike Lamble;
Connell Lee; Peter Mennim; Paul Newton;
Steve Trevaskis; Rod Westblade

Library of Congress
Cataloging-in-Publication Data
Native Americans / consulting editors,
    David Hurst Thomas, Lorann Pendleton.
            p. cm. -- (Discoveries Library)
    Includes index.
    ISBN 0-7835-4759-5
    1. Indians of North America--History--
Juvenile literature. 2. Indians of North
America--Social life and customs--Juvenile
literature. [1. Indians of North America.]
    I. Thomas, David Hurst. II. Pendleton, Lorann
S.A.   III. Series: Discoveries Library
(Alexandria, Va.)
    E77.4.N38 1995
    970.004'97--dc20   95-12101

Manufactured by Mandarin Offset
Printed in China

A Weldon Owen Production

THE NATURE COMPANY
DISCOVERIES
L I B R A R Y

Native Americans

CONSULTING EDITORS

Dr. David Hurst Thomas
Curator, Department of Anthropology
American Museum of Natural History, New York

Lorann Pendleton
Curatorial Assistant, Department of Anthropology
American Museum of Natural History, New York

TIME
LIFE
BOOKS

Contents

Where Did They Come From?

TOOLS
Early Native Americans made knives from stone and bone, which were sharp enough to slice up large animals. They used scrapers to remove the fur and flesh from skins.

Native Americans tell wonderful creation stories to explain where they came from. Some say Coyote shaped people from mud; others think Raven called them from a clam shell because he was lonely. Archaeologists, however, suggest people arrived in several groups, beginning at least 15,000 years ago, perhaps much earlier. The first Americans came from Asia and followed herds of grazing animals across a land bridge formed during the Ice Age, when the great glaciers sucked up the shallow seas and left dry land. Later, when the Earth began to warm, this land bridge disappeared and became the Bering Strait. The people trekked slowly southward into North America through a harsh landscape. They were excellent hunters and speared huge animals such as woolly mammoths and long-horned bison. These enormous beasts later died out, and the people were forced to hunt smaller game and collect wild plants for food.

SHAMAN'S MASK
Many thousands of years ago, an Arctic woodcarver shaped this mask for a shaman (healer) to wear during the ceremonies that called upon the spirits to bring good health and good hunting.

CREATION STORY

The Northeastern Iroquois describe Skywoman's fall from her home. Water birds guided her to an island that a muskrat was building from mud and a turtle's shell. The island grew to become the Earth, and the world began when Skywoman gave birth to a daughter.

HUNTING AND FIGHTING

Early hunters and warriors flaked stone into deadly tips for their spears and lances. They made heavy war clubs from whale bone.

WALK ACROSS THE STRAIT

A strip of water called the Bering Strait now separates Siberia from Alaska. In the Ice Age, when the sea level dropped, the strait became a land bridge for herds of migrating game and the hunters who pursued them.

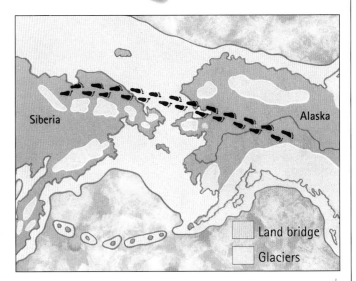

Siberia

Alaska

Land bridge

Glaciers

Discover more in Buffalo Hunters

Where Did They Live?

Tribes of Native Americans spread across the land, depending on nature for food and shelter. Where they lived shaped the way they lived, and each group began to develop different customs and ways of doing things. On the rugged Northwest Coast, the "Salmon and Cedar People" built with wood and ate mainly fish, like their neighbors on the high Plateau. The Inuit (Eskimos) hunted polar bears across the treeless tundra and whales in freezing Arctic waters. Caribou provided nearly everything Subarctic families needed, while buffalo sustained the Plains Indians. In California, the mild climate meant that tribes there had plenty to eat, unlike the parched Great Basin where food was scarce. In the Northeast and Great Lakes, people traveled the rivers and cleared forest plots to grow corn and tobacco. Most Southwest and Southeast tribes became farmers and lived in villages.

Blackfoot medicine man
from the Great Plains

SOUTHWEST LANDSCAPE
A parade of saguaro cactuses in the dry Southwest provided nourishment when the fruit formed and ripened.

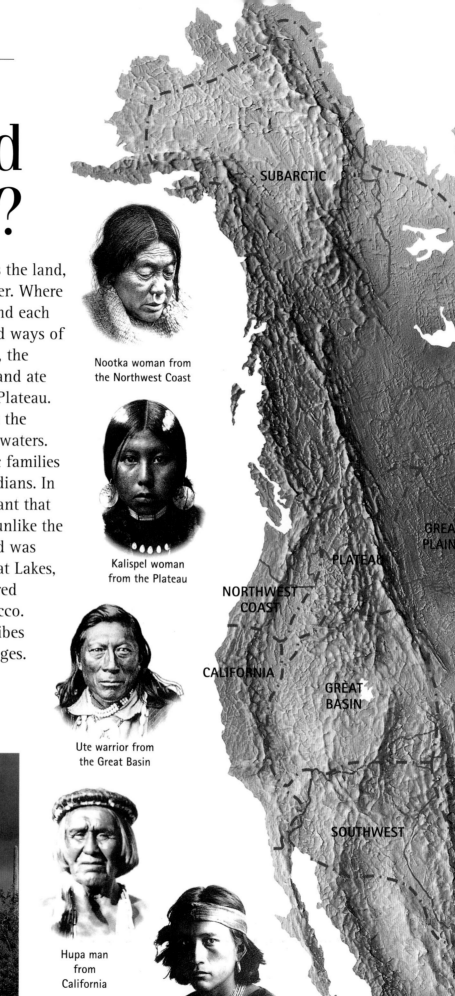

Nootka woman from
the Northwest Coast

Kalispel woman
from the Plateau

Ute warrior from
the Great Basin

Hupa man
from
California

Navajo youth from
the Southwest

SUBARCTIC

GREAT PLAINS

PLATEAU

NORTHWEST COAST

CALIFORNIA

GREAT BASIN

SOUTHWEST

8

ARCTIC

Nunivagmiut man from
the Arctic

SUBARCTIC

WOODLANDS
Trees grew thickly in many areas, and Native
Americans soon began making canoes, weapons,
food containers and other items from wood.

Cree warrior from
the Subarctic

Sauk warrior from
the Northeast

NORTHEAST

SOUTHEAST

Seminole warrior
from the Southeast

SIGN LANGUAGE

As people separated into groups, the way they spoke slowly
changed. Eventually, there were many different languages.
To overcome the problems of not understanding their neighbors,
the tribes on the Great Plains invented sign language— a clever way
of communicating without words. Gesturing with their hands,
chieftains made peace bargains, hunting parties discussed
the whereabouts of game, and Mandan farmers traded
surplus corn for Sioux buffalo skins.

Hello   Riding a horse   Peace   Friend

Discover more in Village Life

9

What Did They Wear?

Native Americans loved decorated ceremonial costumes, but had simple everyday clothes. They dressed to suit the weather on windy plains, in the chill Arctic, in damp rainforests, or in the dry desert, where often they wore very little. Most garments fitted loosely for easy movement—loincloths, shirts, tunics and leggings for men; skirts and dresses for women. In winter, people added shawls, blankets and extra clothing. They made garments from the things around them. Animals provided skins for cloth, sinews for thread and bones for needles. One moose could clothe a person in the Northeast, a single caribou supplied a jacket in the Subarctic, but a man's robe in the Great Basin required a hundred rabbit skins. Where game was scarce, the people wove cloth from plant material, such as nettle fiber and cedar bark.

DRESSED FOR BEST
Both men and women wore ceremonial robes made from soft buckskin, decorated with fringe and porcupine quill embroidery. The brave's full-length war bonnet and coup stick are trimmed with ermine tails and eagle feathers. The feathers show his courage in hand-to-hand fighting.

SNOW GOGGLES
The Inuit (Eskimos) wore goggles shaped from walrus tusk. These protected their eyes from the intense glare of the sun reflected off the snow.

KEEPING WARM
Men, women and children dressed alike against the cold in waterproof pants, hooded parkas, boots and mittens. Caribou and seal skins with the fur turned inside were most popular. Here, the mother chews skin to soften it, while the father carves an ivory ornament with a bow drill.

BARK WEAVING

While her grandchild rocks gently in a cradle, this woman weaves a basket from dampened strips of cedar bark. Her clothing is also woven from shredded bark. Cedar bark was one of the main plant fibers used by the people of the Northwest Coast.

FOOTWEAR

Plains women stitched leather moccasins with hard or soft soles. They decorated them with dyed porcupine quills and elaborate beadwork.

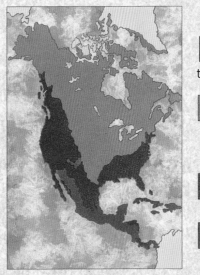

CLOTHING MATERIALS

Native Americans made their clothing from the animal and plant materials they found around them.

Areas where animal fur (such as caribou, seal and polar bear) and hide (such as buckskin and buffalo) were used for clothing.

Areas where cotton was mainly used for clothing.

Areas where both animal skins and plant materials were used for clothing.

Discover more in Getting Around

11

Life as a Child

Children spent most of the first year of their lives strapped snugly in a cradleboard, carried everywhere by their mothers. Later, a large family of parents, aunts, uncles and grandparents watched over them and taught them tribal ways. Girls practiced preparing food, sewing, tanning hides, making pottery, basket weaving and embroidering with dyed porcupine quills. Boys learned to make tools and weapons and how to hunt and fight. There was always time for games, such as hurtling down snowy slopes on sleds made from buffalo ribs. When children reached puberty, there were important ceremonies, sometimes with dancing, special clothes and the gift of a new name. Apache girls were showered with yellow tule pollen; Alaskan girls had their faces tattooed. After puberty, girls joined the women in the tribe, but boys had to pass tests of courage, such as wounding or killing an enemy, before they could become true hunters and warriors.

UMBILICAL POUCHES
Some tribes sewed newborn babies' umbilical cords into beaded pouches shaped like lizards or turtles. They believed these creatures would bless their infants with long life.

TARGET PRACTICE
Sioux boys learned how to use small bows and arrows, shooting first at still targets and then at moving jack rabbits.

UNDER THE STARS
Like Native American children everywhere, the boys and girls of the Great Basin gathered to hear stories. The retelling of myths, legends and folktales taught the children tribal history and customs.

DRESSING WARM
St. Lawrence Island children in the Arctic wore parkas made from reindeer skin with the hairy side on the inside. The tops of boys' heads were shaved like the men of the tribe. Girls kept their hair long.

CRADLEBOARD

This Cheyenne cradleboard was made of beaded cotton lashed securely to a wooden frame. It fitted comfortably on the mother's back.

BRIDAL NECKLACE
A Zuni man made this silver and turquoise necklace for his daughter. The traditional squash blossom design represented a mother surrounded by her many children.

Choosing a Partner

Some Native American couples began life together with a simple exchange of presents. Then the girl (perhaps no more than 13 years old) moved into her husband's home, or he joined her family. Subarctic partners set up a wigwam together. Marriage ceremonies varied greatly between tribes and regions. The richest of the Northwest Coast Tlingits gave huge wedding feasts and valuable presents. A Plains boy courted his sweetheart with fluted love tunes. In the evening, outside her tepee, the couple hid from curious passers-by with a blanket over their heads, while they chatted to see if they liked each other. In later times, wealthy Plains bridegrooms gave horses to the bride's family. Southwestern Hopis sealed their marriage partnership when the mothers washed their hair together in one bowl.

WISHRAM BRIDE
A Wishram bride on the high Plateau wore wedding finery made from panels of dentalium shells, edged with beads and coins.

READY FOR MARRIAGE
A Hopi girl's elaborate hairstyle indicated to a Hopi boy that she was old enough to be married.

MARRIAGE DOLLS
Menominee newlyweds near the Great Lakes received a pair of dolls as a wedding present. These were "good medicine" for a long and happy marriage.

14

ACROSS THE WATER

This Kwakiutl bride arrived at her future husband's village in the family canoe.

WEDDING BASKETS

Navajo wedding baskets always belonged to the bride. When a man moved into his wife's home, he looked after her goods but never owned them himself.

READY FOR MARRIAGE

A Hopi boy wore several fine bead necklaces on his wedding day.

Hopi Wedding

A Hopi bride ground corn for three days in her chosen partner's house to show her wifely skills. After the hair-washing ceremony, she stayed there while the groom and his male relatives wove her wedding clothes. Then she walked home in one outfit, carrying the second one in a reed container. Women were buried in their wedding garments so that when they entered the spirit world, they would be properly dressed.

Wedding blanket sash

Games and Sport

Many tribes played stickball or lacrosse (shown here) to settle quarrels and to ask the spirits to send rain or to heal a sick person. The game was fast and violent, and players in the Southeast called it "the little brother of war." Competitors were sometimes severely injured or even killed during the game. The spectators chanted and cheered to urge the players on and bet furs, skins and trinkets on the results. Sports helped the men develop their hunting and fighting skills, such as strength, courage, staying power, swiftness and keenness of eye. As well as team games, there were running, canoe and horse races, spear throwing and archery contests. In some tribes, women also played active sports. But most of all, people throughout the land loved to gamble. Games of chance included guessing which way up peach kernels or walnut shells would land in a bowl, which hand held a marked bone or which moccasin contained a small stone.

PLAYING CARDS
Both Apache men and women enjoyed card games. The packs of cards were cut from rawhide and painted with bold designs.

DID YOU KNOW?
Sioux women bet on the fall of dice made from bones, beavers' teeth and other materials, which were carved and painted with spiders, lizards or turtles.

ARCTIC KICKBALL
Arctic tribes played kickball with a leather ball stuffed with caribou fur.

PLAYING PATOL

Patol is a game of chance played by two to four people. They use counters called "horses," stick dice and stones arranged in a circle or rectangle. Players become very skilful at throwing the dice. Patol was popular in the Southwest, where games took place outside in front of interested onlookers.

RING AND PIN
In this game, players held the wooden pin and tried to pass the loop of string over the deer-foot bones.

GAMBLING GAME
The sticks in this game were shuffled under a cover and divided into two bundles. Players then guessed which bundle contained a specially marked stick.

Hoop

Lance

HOOP AND POLE GAME
This was a game of great skill. Competitors had to throw a lance through a hoop as it rolled along the ground. A hit on the center hole scored the most points.

Canoes and Kayaks

People built boats for fishing, moving between hunting grounds, carrying goods and going to war. Some hollowed out massive tree trunks with fire, others wove crafts from reeds, or covered wooden frames with birch bark and sealed the seams with hot black spruce gum. Low-ended crafts steered best in calm waters. Boats with high bows and sterns resisted rough waves and were more suitable for the open ocean. The tall prow of a ceremonial Northwest Coast canoe (shown here) was carved and painted to reflect the family's importance. The fearsome bear is a villager dressed in his winter dance costume. The Californian Chumash put to sea in canoes built from pine planks. Inuit (Eskimos) made lightweight, waterproof kayaks, by stretching oiled animal skins over driftwood frames. Most kayaks were for one person, though some held two.

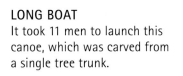

LONG BOAT
It took 11 men to launch this canoe, which was carved from a single tree trunk.

HUNTING CRAFT
Inuit hunters stalked sea mammals in their speedy, silent kayaks.

18

PADDLE POWER
The helmsman used a broad-bladed oar. The crew propelled the boat through the water with shorter, more pointed blades. Patterns on the paddles matched the canoe's decoration.

TULE BOAT
In Northern California, fishers skimmed across the lakes in boats made from bundles of tule reeds, lashed together. These reeds grew plentifully near water.

BIRCH BARK CANOE
Sheets of paper birch bark, sewn together, formed the best covering. The resin in the bark stopped it from stretching or shrinking.

MAKING A DUGOUT CANOE
Northwest Coast people used the sea as both hunting ground and trade route. They built one kind of canoe for the calmer waters of the bay and another for the open ocean.

The cedar log was split lengthwise. Shaping began with a stone tool.

The sides were chipped away to reach the required thickness.

Hollowing the inside to the correct thickness took skill and time.

Water heated with hot rocks softened the wood. Thwarts were fitted to broaden the interior.

The bow and stern pieces were attached, and the hull was sanded and decorated.

TOY CANOE
This birch bark model is engraved all over, unlike a full-sized canoe, which was not decorated on the bottom.

BULLBOAT
Mandan women rowed bullboats made from buffalo hides stretched over frames of willow.

DOG SLEDDING

The inventive Arctic tribes trained huskies to pull sleds. They laid a platform of driftwood or caribou antlers on wooden or whalebone runners. The Netsilik sometimes used rolled animal skins for runners, with frozen fish as crosspieces—a handy food supply in the spring thaw.

Getting Around

Native Americans walked huge distances in their never-ending quest for food. Apaches painted their moccasins with sacred tule pollen because they believed it would help them find their way. Possessions had to be carried, and woven baskets were popular containers. A broad band, called a tumpline, held the load on the back of the human carrier. Women took the heaviest burdens and backpacked babies, tied tightly in slings or cradleboards. Men seldom carried anything but weapons, because they always had to be ready to hunt or to defend the group. The Subarctic people hauled packs on toboggans. In other places, people harnessed dogs to wooden travois or loaded them with parfleches. Later, horses and pack ponies made life easier for the tribes who had them.

PIGGYBACKING

Young children, like this Hopi toddler, rode on their mother's back. This was a comfortable and safe way of carrying them for long distances where there were no sleds or toboggans.

TANGLE FREE

Ivory separators and swivels kept harness lines on dog sleds from becoming tangled.

DOG TRAVOIS

A tough dog could pull a load about equal in weight to two medium-sized suitcases full of clothes.

DID YOU KNOW?

One legend explained that baskets walked by themselves until Coyote, the mischievous wolf spirit, said they looked silly. He made women carry them from then on.

SNOWSHOE SHUFFLE

Snowshoes, shaped like bear paws or beaver tails, were the perfect winter footwear for journeying through deep snow drifts. They allowed hunters to keep pace with caribou and other large game without their feet sinking into the soft snow. Subarctic tribes laced bent frames of birchwood with strips of wet caribou hide. When the webbing dried, it was tight and light.

PLAIN AND SIMPLE

The Southeastern Seminoles made their moccasins from a single piece of soft buckskin gathered at the seam.

WALKING WARM

In summer, Eskimos gathered grasses and braided them into socks. They were shaped to fit the foot snugly.

HUSKY HELPERS

Husky dogs pulled sleds in teams. They also used their keen noses to track down seals for the hunters.

Discover more in Tepees

Horses and Ponies

SADDLE BLANKET
Respected horses were as
well-dressed as their owners.
It took many hours to edge
this blanket with beads.

Horses brought speed to the Plains Indians and changed their hunting and fighting ways. They were called "Spirit Dogs" or "Medicine Dogs," but were much stronger and faster pack animals than real dogs. With horses, whole settlements could move freely to follow the buffalo. The hunter–warrior had a special bond with his horse; only he trained and rode it, bathed it in summer, covered it with buffalo skins in winter and tethered it beside his tepee. Horses, extinct since the Ice Age, were reintroduced by the Spanish in the sixteenth century and spread gradually from tribe to tribe. The Plains Comanches excelled in taming wild horses. Comanche women joined the men on antelope hunts, and the children rode solo by the age of five. Plateau tribes bred Appaloosa horses and Indian ponies and became expert horse traders.

WHIPS AND QUIRTS
Whips or quirts urged horses
on. This quirt is made
from an elk antler
and a leather strip.

STRANGERS ON HORSEBACK
This Navajo cave painting of a Spanish friar and his companions has survived from the sixteenth century.

SADDLE UP
Men usually rode bareback. Women used saddles and stirrups. Crow women spent many hours trimming theirs with beads.

Saddle pommel

Stirrup

SADDLE BAG
Bags were made from deerskin, stitched up the sides. They were tied to the pommel of the saddle.

TAILPIECE
A crupper passed from the back of the saddle under the horse's tail to keep the saddle from slipping.

BATTLEDRESS

Plains warriors depended on their war horses. The animals' reactions in battle could mean the difference between life and death. They had to endure the noise, move quickly, turn sharply and respond instantly to their riders' commands. Warriors shared battle honors with their mounts and painted them with the symbols they used on their own bodies (below). The horses wore eagle feathers and scalp locks, and their manes and tails were often trimmed and dyed.

Plains pony

Appaloosa horse

War party leader

Enemy killed in hand combat

Hail

Mourning marks

Discover more in Life on a Reservation

The Foragers

From early spring to late autumn, many Native American tribes moved around frequently, searching for things to eat. They foraged for seeds, berries, nuts and roots. In the Great Basin, March cattail shoots were the first fresh vegetables, while September's pine nuts provided needed stores for winter. Occasional grasshopper plagues were tasty feasts. The men caught almost anything, from rats, mice, caterpillars and lizards, to larger game including jack rabbits and deer. They made lifelike decoys from reeds and feathers to lure wild ducks into shallow water. Then they grabbed the birds or shot them down with arrows. In California, foragers hunted in the mountains and on the sea coast. They harvested acorns from oak trees and ground them into flour.

SEED HARVESTING
When the seeds ripened, Californian women beat them straight from the bushes into their carrying baskets.

The summer sun ripened fruits, nuts and berries, and tribes knew where to find them in their region. The foragers dried some of these and put them aside for winter, when food was often in very short supply.

Persimmons

Cranberries

Black walnut

Buffalo berries

Pine nuts

WICKER LARDER
The foragers used woven baskets to collect, store and carry food. These were much lighter than containers made from clay and were not easily broken.

A DIFFICULT CATCH
The sure-footed bighorn sheep that browsed in the desert mountains provided a satisfying meal. Men, women and children banded together to trap the animals.

Discover more in Buffalo Hunters

WAFFLE GARDENS
Small clay compartments,
resembling the sections of
a waffle, held water from the
nearby river. The Southwest
Zuni grew melons, herbs,
tomatoes, chilies and onions
in these waffle gardens.

Sunflowers

• MAKING A LIVING •

The Farmers

The Southeast, parts of the Southwest, and the
eastern edge of the Plains were the best areas for
farming. Tribes grew corn, wheat, fruits and garden
vegetables, often using clever methods, such as planting
beans beside growing corn so the beans climbed the
cornstalks for support. Farmers invented ways to water the
land, scare birds from ripening crops, keep mice and moisture
out of stored grain, and stop the soil from being
overused. They believed supernatural beings
controlled their farming fortunes, so they performed
rituals for healthy harvests. Southwest Papagos
drank syrup from the saguaro cactus
and danced for rain. Nearby,
Pueblo tribes told how Blue Corn
Woman and White Corn
Maiden brought corn to
Earth. Newborn Pueblo
babies still receive ears of
corn for good luck.

LIVING OFF THE LAND
Wild plants that yielded seeds
and fruit, such as gourds, pumpkins,
sunflowers and cob corn, later
became cultivated crops.

Dried gourd

DESERT PLANTING
Corn seeds were planted deep enough for their root systems to reach underground moisture.

HOPI CORN FIELD
Small patches of Hopi corn thrived on the desert slopes. The plants were well adapted to the harsh, dry conditions.

FARMING TOOLS
Hidatsa farmers made rakes from deer antlers and hoes from buffalo shoulder bones, attached to wooden handles with strips of sinew.

Acorn squash

Dried corn

THE SEASON FOR SEEDS

The Bean Dance, a February ritual, lasted for 16 days. Masked dancers prayed for strong seed growth and acted as rain-giving kachina spirits. During this time, Hopi children learned about their religion.

Discover more in Making a Meal

Club

HALIBUT
FISHING TACKLE
The Tlingits carved hooks to catch halibut. They stunned the heavy fish with clubs before hauling them into the boat.

Hook

HARPOONING WALRUSES
Hunting walruses was dangerous but worthwhile. They provided meat, skin for boats and clothing, and ivory tusks for ornaments and utensils.

• MAKING A LIVING •

The Fishers

In late spring, salmon begin to race up the inland waterways to lay their eggs. The Northwestern tribes thought they came especially to provide their people with food, and caught them in nets and traps. They offered prayers to the first salmon landed, roasted it for everyone to taste, and returned the whole skeleton to the river where, they believed, it would come alive again. The ocean was also a rich source of food for these people. From it, they took whales, seals, huge halibut, cod and sturgeon, all kinds of shellfish and oily candlefish, which gave them fuel for lamps. Other tribes speared fish by torchlight from their canoes on the Great Lakes and used nets and traps during the day. In parts of the Southeast, the people depended on fish, as well as turtles, alligators and deer, for protein in their diet. The Inuit (Eskimos) needed meat from sea mammals to survive in winter when they had no plant food. They caught seals and stalked walruses among the ice floes.

DID YOU KNOW?
The Inuit (Eskimos) divided their world into land and sea things. They would not eat the flesh of land and sea animals in the same meal or cook caribou meat over a driftwood fire.

NET GAUGE

Twine to make mesh fishing nets was wound around a rectangular gauge. This one is made from elk antlers.

WHALING IN A UMIAK

Whales were dangerous prey. Arctic tribes went after them in single-sailed rowing boats called umiaks. They were made from whalebone covered with walrus hides and waterproofed with seal oil. Umiaks were much stronger than kayaks. Inuit (Eskimo) fishers sometimes hunted bowhead whales that were twice as long as the boats. They caught smaller beluga whales for their skin and tusked narwhals for their oil.

Whaling float

TRAPPING FISH

The Ingalik people of the Subarctic set wheel fish traps beneath the ice. Large ones, like this, were mainly used for snaring ling, a cod-like fish.

ULU KNIFE

Women butchered meat, scraped skins and cut leather with an ulu. It had a slate blade and a bone, ivory or wood handle.

Discover more in Canoes and Kayaks

33

Making a Meal

Imagine making a meal with no tap water, no gas or electricity and no refrigeration and supermarkets. Native Americans had none of these, and the women spent hours collecting food and water and preparing things to eat. Their daughters worked alongside them from a very early age. Pueblo women baked corn bread in outdoor ovens. The Northwestern Tlingits filled baskets of closely woven spruce roots with water, meat and vegetables, dropped in hot stones till the water boiled, and made a stew. Plains Indians used buffalo-hide containers in the same way. Metal cooking pots, which lasted much longer than skin or woven ones, became popular after tribes began trading with the Europeans. Native Americans had no set meal times. People ate when they were hungry, after a good hunt or when travelers arrived. Sharing was very important. Plenty of food meant lots for everyone. If provisions were in short supply, the small amounts were divided evenly. Most tribes stored food for the winter, when plants and game were harder to find.

PLENTY ON THE PLAINS
During most of the year, there was plenty to eat on the Plains. These Cheyenne women are pounding wild cherries and cooking with hot stones and metal pots. Turnips and squash will be added to the stew.

DRYING CHILIES
Chili peppers were a popular crop in the Southwest and gave the food a hot, spicy flavor. The pods were strung on plant fibers or cotton cords and hung up to dry.

SUN-DRIED FOODS

When food was plentiful, it could be preserved for winter. Fish, meat, corn, fruit and vegetables were hung on racks or spread out on platforms to dry in the sun.

IN STORAGE

Large storage jars for food were woven from willow wood and sedge roots. They were patterned with darker plants, such as devil's claw, or decorated with brightly colored feathers.

GRINDING CORN

Most days young Hopi women gathered to grind corn. They placed the corn kernels on a rough stone slab called a "metate" and rubbed them with a smaller stone called a "mano." Then they moved the pieces to progressively smoother slabs and crushed them into finer and finer particles. The Hopi cooked cornmeal flour in several ways. They made it into more than 30 different dishes including bread, gruel, pancakes and dumplings.

Discover more in Village Life

35

Village Life

Living in villages meant safety in numbers and shared supplies. Some groups built permanent dwellings. Others followed the food trails, like the Subarctic people who carried caribou skin shelters from camp to camp. Several tribes wintered in pit houses covered with mud. Alaskan Eskimos lived partly underground beneath turf roofs, while Southeastern Seminoles raised their thatched homes on stilts above the swampy land. Southwesterners solved the problem of fitting many people into a small space by stacking their stone and mud-brick houses one on top of another, like modern apartment buildings. Native American dwellings came in various shapes: cones, domes, triangles, squares and rectangles. Their names were just as varied: chickees, hogans, igloos, tepees, longhouses, lean-tos, wigwams and wickiups.

ROUND HOUSES
The Mandan people built villages on rises beside the Missouri River. Heavy rain ran easily down the domed sides of the houses.

PUEBLO VILLAGE
Southwestern villages were honeycombs of two-storey stone houses. Ladders led to the roofs and the entrances to the upper rooms.

SPLIT LEVEL LIVING
Up to 12 Northeastern Iroquois families shared a longhouse. The top level was used for storage, the bottom for sleeping. Curtains separated areas.

VILLAGE LAYOUT

In the well-planned Creek villages of the Southeast, airy summer sleepouts were built beside warmer lodges. The largest round council buildings could seat 500 people. The villagers used them for ceremonies, dancing, winter meetings of the tribal elders and to house the homeless and the aged.

FRONT DOOR POLES
Northwest Coast tribes, such as the Haida, lived in wooden buildings. Carved cedar totem poles indicated who lived in each house.

BARK SHELTER
Some tribes built huts from chunks of redwood or cedar bark. The sweet-smelling wood repelled insects.

Discover more in Tepees

Tepees

The Plains Indians lived in cone-shaped structures called tepees, made out of buffalo hides sewn together. When tribes needed to move on to find food or to escape from enemies, they could fold the tepees and transport them easily. At first, they carried their belongings on dog travois, so tepees were limited in size to the height of a man. Later, when horses were used for transportation, the tepees became much bigger. The space inside these portable homes was very limited, and the furniture was simple and functional. Buffalo skins made comfortable bedding. Backrests of willow rods laced together with string and supported by poles formed chairs, which could be rolled up neatly. Rawhide saddlebags called "parfleches" doubled as cushions or pillows. Tepees were erected with the steeper, rear side against the westerly winds, and the doorway facing east, towards the rising sun. In the windy areas of the southern plains, the Sioux and Cheyenne supported their tepees with three foundation poles, while further north, the Hidatsa, Crow and Blackfeet used four poles. Ceremonial and larger tepees had more supports.

TEPEE DECORATION
Ornaments were tied to the top of the tepee poles. These are leather thongs wrapped in grass and tipped with yarn tufts.

Family possessions
Families kept everything they owned inside their tepee. It was kitchen, bedroom, playroom, living room and shed all in the one space.

Symbols of the Blackfeet
Painted symbols, such as rainbow stripes or a buffalo head, protected the tepee owners against sickness and bad luck.

RESERVATION CAMP
When the Plains Indians were forced to move to reservations by the United States government, they took their tepees with them and pitched them in tribal groups. They tried to preserve as much of the way of life from their homelands as possible.

Smoke flaps
These could be opened from the inside with a pair of long poles.

TEPEE CAMPS

Tepee camps were pitched in a C shape with the opening facing east. Behavior inside the tepee followed strict rules. An open door was a sign of welcome. Men entered to the right, women to the left. Younger men remained silent until they were invited to speak. No one walked between the fire and another person. Visitors brought their own bowls, and when the host cleaned his pipe, it was time for visitors to leave.

N

Dew cloth
A decorated lining called a dew cloth was tied inside the tepee. It kept out moisture and helped to insulate the tepee.

BUFFALO SKIN
Hides were tanned and smoked so that they would be waterproof but still remain soft. Some were decorated for ceremonial tepees or painted with a family clan's symbol.

Lacing
The tepee was laced from the bottom to the smoke hole with pins carved from flexible willow wood.

Entrance
The door was made from a flap of skin and was oval or V-shaped.

Fireplace
The fire was placed under the smoke hole, and the woodpile was near the door.

Hemline
The hem was pegged to the ground with stakes but raised in hot weather to let in air.

COMPACT CARVING
Totem pole carvers used pictures to tell stories. They compressed images of symbolic creatures, such as those shown here, into small spaces.

SUN MASK
This Bella Coola mask was worn during winter ceremonies. The central symbol represents the spirit of the life-giving sun.

THUNDERBIRD MASK
Kwakiutl masks sometimes had movable parts. When the pieces of this bird's beak swing open, they reveal a human mask.

• CEREMONIES AND RITUALS •

Totems, Masks and Kachinas

On the Northwest Coast, woodcarvers turned cedar trees into totem poles to record the history of a family or an important person. Figures of animals, such as Sea Grizzly Bear, and mythical creatures, such as Thunderbird, told of clans' connections with their spirit ancestors. These characters were easily recognized. Raven clan's symbol was a bird's head with a straight beak; Eagle clan's emblem had a beak that curved. Totem artists also carved masks for storytelling and rituals. The wearers took on the power of the spirits that the masks represented. Tribes in other regions used masks, too. The Southwest Hopis had dozens of kachina masks. In the Northeast, the Iroquoian False Face Society wore elaborate wood and horsehair masks and the Husk Face Society whispered fortunes through cornhusk masks.

KACHINA DOLLS

Southwestern tribes, such as the Zuni and the Hopi, carved kachina dolls out of wood. They clothed them in masks and costumes to look exactly like the men who dressed up as kachina spirits. These dolls were not playthings. They were given to the children to teach them to identify the many different kachinas and the parts they played in tribal ceremonies.

Zuni kachina doll

TODAY'S TOTEM ART
Thunderbird, on top of this modern totem, is the carver's personal crest and shows he belongs to a Kwakiutl warrior group.

DOGFISH MASK
A dancer wearing this dogfish mask pulled a string to make the figure riding the dorsal fin twirl.

SEA OTTER MASK
The curved arms around the sea otter's head whirl around and support birds with flapping cloth wings.

41

Special Occasions

Native Americans enjoyed many special occasions. They celebrated important times in people's lives, such as reaching the age of puberty, getting married or being successful in battle. Ceremonial clothing, decorated with fur, feathers, quilling and beadwork, was worn for these events, and people made necklaces, earrings and bracelets from animal teeth, bones and claws, shells and stones. Native Americans believed that the sky, the soil, plants, birds, animals, rivers and everything else had spirits that must be respected. These spirits could be reached through dance, song, prayer and other religious rituals. Some tribes also worshipped monsters, such as the dreadful Cannibal Spirit of the Northwest, and danced to show their evil power.

SACRED ROOM
The underground "kiva" was the holy place of Southwest kachina priests. The chamber's floor became an altar when it was sprinkled with cornmeal, sand, ground bark and flowers.

DRESSED TO DANCE
Kwakiutl shamans wore cedar bark costumes and painted wooden masks to represent the birdlike friends of the fearsome Cannibal Spirit.

CANNIBAL SPIRIT DANCERS
The Cannibal Spirit dancer is standing on the left wearing a cedar bark ring around his neck. His fearsome followers squat in front.

FAMILY JEWELRY
Navajo women wore ear pendants before marriage. Afterwards, they attached them to bead necklaces until their own daughters were old enough to wear them.

FEATHER HEADDRESS
Ceremonial costumes made from eagle feathers, like this chieftain's war bonnet, had special importance. Eagles were linked with heavenly spirits and admired for their speed, fierceness and sharp eyesight.

POLLEN RITUAL
A blessing of pollen, the tribe's most powerful "medicine," is a highlight of the four-day puberty ritual for an Apache girl. Baskets of yellow pollen from tule rushes are gathered for the ceremony. The grains are then sprinkled over the girl's hair and face.

Pollen basket

Discover more in Pipes and Powwows

SNOWSHOE DANCER
An Objibwa hunter rejoices after the first winter snowfall. Now his prey will flounder in drifts and be much easier to catch.

FLUTED MELODY
Flute music, called the "wind that breathes life into the heart," accompanied many dances. The six round holes represented the Earth, sky and the four directions: north, south, east and west.

MARKING TIME
This rattle has a dried gourd body, a handle covered in glass beads and streamers made from feathers and strips of sinew.

Ceremonial Dancing

Ceremonial dancing was the Native American way of celebrating joyous occasions and praying for health, successful hunting and good harvests. Plains Sioux imitated the sounds and movements of bears before the hunt or whooped in a scalp dance after a battle victory. The Californian Patwin tribe danced in huge headdresses and cloaks made of feathers or grass to encourage the growth of wild crops. Hopi men in the dry Southwest collected snakes for an elaborate ritual. The snake priests, wearing feathered headdresses and kilts patterned with the serpent motif, circled the village square with the reptiles in their mouths. Their companions stroked the creatures with eagle feathers to stop them from biting. The snakes were then returned to the desert where their lightning-like, zigzag movements were supposed to bring pre-harvest rain.

KACHINA SPIRITS

Hopi men impersonated kachinas, important spirits in their religion. They performed dances during the seasons of seed sowing, plant growth and harvesting. Kachina dancers taught young children tribal ways and gave them dolls.

Kachina doll

RATTLING RHYTHM

Inuit (Eskimo) men wore sealskin gauntlet gloves for ceremonial dancing. This pair is decorated with horned puffin beaks and quills from feathers, which rattled to the beat of the drum.

TAPPING RHYTHM

An Inuit (Eskimo) woodcarver made this baton. The woodpecker is attached to the shaft with springy whale cartilage. During the dance, it pecks like a real bird.

45

Pipes and Powwows

Native Americans used solemn pipe-smoking rituals to ask for the spirits' help to make war, peace or rain, to hunt successfully, or to seal a good trade bargain. Pipes were very special and very beautiful. Each one took several weeks to make. The stem was hollow wood, and the bowl was fashioned from soft soapstone, clay or wood. Supernatural powers did not flow through the pipe until these two parts were ceremonially joined. In the past, pipes were smoked at powwows where people gathered to pray for the sick or for the tribe's success in battle or hunting. Today, powwows are joyful events, held at least once a year, to remind people of old customs and to celebrate new ones.

TOBACCO BAG
The pipe bowl, the pipe stem and the smoking mixture were kept in a quilled and beaded buckskin pouch.

PIPE CEREMONY
Ceremonial pipe smoking had special importance. As one Sioux tribesman explained: "This pipe is us. The stem is our backbone, the bowl our head. The stone is our blood, red as our skin."

PIPE TOMAHAWK
Pipe tomahawks with sharp steel blades and inlaid handles were prized ceremonial objects, rather than weapons of war.

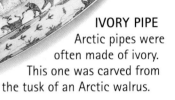

IVORY PIPE
Arctic pipes were often made of ivory. This one was carved from the tusk of an Arctic walrus.

PRAYER RITUAL
A Sioux warrior placed a buffalo skull at his feet and pointed his pipe skyward while he prayed for supernatural powers.

TOBACCO PLANT
Tobacco was believed to have magical powers to heal or to hurt, to change people's fortunes, or to call up good spirits and drive away evil.

THE POWWOW CIRCUITS

The original powwows were meetings of Plains Indians. Now these celebrations of Indian life and tradition are held in Canada and the United States, from the Pacific Northwest to the Atlantic. In cities, the venue is a large gymnasium or open park. In the country, powwow organizers set up special grounds. Performers of traditional dances spend the summer months traveling the powwow circuit. These cheerful, colorful festivities also involve singers, craftspeople, families, friends and the local community.

Northwest drum

Discover more in The Future

47

Healers and Healing

Calling a doctor was no simple matter for Native Americans. Often, visits and ceremonial treatments lasted for several days. They were organized by healers, known as shamans or medicine men and women, some of whom had as much power as any chief. Shamans cured the sick with herbs, performed healing rituals, told the future or found missing property. They knew the dances, chants, prayers and ceremonies that would bring good fortune to their tribes and please the spirits. Young people had to take many difficult tests of physical strength before they could become shamans, and few succeeded. They did not receive their special powers until they had seen a vision in the form of a sacred animal or object. Native Americans were generally very healthy until fatal diseases were introduced from Europe.

MEDICINE KIT
A Sioux woman once owned this rawhide bag of medicines. The wrapped bundles contained crushed leaves and powdered bark and roots.

SWEAT LODGES
Skins over a wooden frame made an airtight hut. Inside, water poured on hot stones turned to steam, like a modern sauna. Warriors cleansed their bodies and the sick eased fevers and aching bones.

PRAYER SNAKES
Some tribes thought that snakes caused stomach complaints. To cure such gastric upsets, Navajo medicine men made snake-shaped prayer sticks from wood and feathers.

DRY SAND PAINTING

Navajo healers used powdered rocks to create large pictures on the floor of the patient's dwelling. They believed the sand could absorb evil sickness. After the ritual, they destroyed the painting.

TOOL OF TRADE

Rattles were an essential part of the Tlingit shaman's ritual equipment. This one's wild hair, beard and mustache are made from human hair.

Q: What did Navajos use to cure stomach complaints?

HONORED HEALER

Slow Bull, photographed on the Plains with a sacred buffalo skull, was a well-respected Oglala Sioux medicine man.

HERBS AND FLOWERS

Native Americans used many herbal medicines. From willow bark they extracted a pain-relieving ingredient, used in today's aspirin. Southeastern Cherokees believed every plant would cure a specific sickness. Iris roots ground with suet, lard and beeswax made an ointment for cuts and grazes. Juice of lady's slipper roots eased pain, soothed hysterics and relieved colds and flu.

Wild purple iris

Yellow lady's slipper

49

FOE KILLED
The Sioux clipped and dyed feathers to count special coups. A red spot indicated the wearer had killed his foe.

SINGLE WOUND
A feather dyed red meant the wearer had been wounded in battle.

MANY COUPS
A jagged edge proclaimed that the wearer had felled several enemies.

MANY WOUNDS
Split feathers were a sign that the wearer had been wounded many times.

FOE SCALPED
A notched feather showed the wearer had cut his enemy's throat and then taken his scalp.

THROAT CUT
The top of the feather clipped diagonally signaled that the wearer had cut his foe's throat without scalping him.

GREAT WARRIOR
Braves who fought well became respected war leaders and were entitled to wear elaborate ceremonial costumes.

• A CHANGING WORLD •

Warriors and Warfare

Some Native American tribes hated war, but many fought constantly over land and horses, to avenge their people and to rack up battle honors. They carried out hit-and-run raids more often than full-scale warfare. Sometimes they adopted prisoners; other times they tortured or scalped them. Southeastern men wore loincloths and moccasins on the warpath and carried weapons and moccasin repair kits. The men walked in single file, and stepped in the footprints of the warrior in front. Chickasaw scouts tied bear paws to their feet to lay confusing trails. Northeasterners stalked the woodlands, signaling to each other with animal calls, or clashed in canoes on the Great Lakes. Plains warriors considered hand-to-hand fighting more courageous and skillful than firing arrows from a distance. A brave proclaimed his "coup" (French for "blow") score by attaching golden eagle tail feathers to his war bonnet and ceremonial robe.

WAR SHIELDS
Warriors prized their buffalo hide shields. Some were covered with deerskin and decorated with symbolic animals, bells and feathers.

TROPHIES OF WAR

In some tribes, scalps brought honor to the warrior who took them. In others, counting coups or capturing horses from the enemy were much more important. Native Americans believed the scalp contained a person's soul and that spiritual power flowed from the slain warrior to the victorious brave. After a successful battle, many tribes danced through the night around the scalps of their foes. They preserved these war trophies by stretching them over a wooden hoop attached to a stick.

WAR WHISTLE
When a Mandan warrior saw an enemy, he blew a whistle like this, which is made from bone wrapped in porcupine quills.

BOWS AND ARROWS
Warriors carried their tightly strung bows and sharp arrows in tanned leather cases.

Arrival of Strangers

In 1492, Caribbean islanders saw Columbus's ships approaching. They thought they came from the sky, home of powerful spirits. Columbus inspired adventurous Europeans from the "Old World" to visit America, the "New World." People from Spain, England, France and Russia came in search of land, minerals and furs. Some tried to convert the tribes to their religion; others used them as slaves. Europe acquired trade goods and new foods, such as chocolate, sunflowers, corn and peanuts; Native Americans gained guns, horses, metal tools and whiskey. Old and New worlds did not mix well. White settlers often took land by force and shot thousands of buffalo for sport. Native Americans, who shared most things and wasted little, could not understand this behavior. One old man despaired, "When the buffalo went away, the hearts of my people fell to the ground, and they could not lift them up again."

CHRISTIAN MISSIONARIES
The Spanish brought Christianity and hard labor to the Southeast, Southwest and California. Many Native Americans died from new diseases and harsh treatment.

MEETING OF CULTURES
Spanish soldiers first met Southeastern tribes in the sixteenth century. They reported that the region was "good for bread and wine and all sorts of livestock."

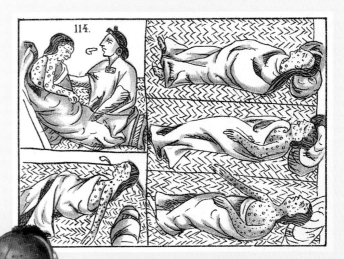

DEADLY DISEASES

Most Native Americans lived a clean, uncrowded, outdoor life and were very healthy. They had no built-in resistance to European infectious diseases, and thousands died of smallpox, measles, typhus, mumps, chickenpox, tuberculosis, influenza, cholera and other illnesses.

CHRISTIAN SYMBOLS
Native Americans who adopted Christianity were often buried with crosses and other religious emblems.

CLUES FROM THE PAST
Coins, medals and other small metal objects belonging to sixteenth-century Spanish settlers tell archaeologists how these people lived.

DID YOU KNOW?
European traders exchanged mass-produced shell beads, known as "wampum", for valuable fur skins, such as sea otter pelts.

RATION TICKETS
Government agents brought
rations of beef, flour and
other food to the reservations.
There was seldom enough to
go around.

• A CHANGING WORLD •

Life on a Reservation

When Europeans began to colonize America, they fought bitterly with the Native Americans over land. In 1830, President Jackson passed a law saying that the government could set up areas in the west called reservations. These were exchanged for tribal homelands, which the new settlers wanted to farm. Native Americans were not allowed to argue their case in the law courts. When they resisted being moved, many people, including United States soldiers, died in the struggles to drive Native American families from their homes. The Southeastern tribes were forced to walk the "Trail of Tears" to the west. Some arrived without food, mules, plows or building materials. Thousands of Native Americans perished from hunger and misery. Although reservation schools taught the ways of white people, Native Americans never forgot where they had come from, and children learned their own customs from their parents and grandparents.

GOVERNMENT PROMISES
This letter from the
government, dated 1838,
granted reservation land
to the Cherokees but kept
the right to build
roads and forts
within the area.

THE TRAIL OF TEARS
Bluecoat soldiers marched
16,000 Cherokees along
"the trail where they
cried." Two thousand died
along the way, and
another 2,000 died soon
after the long journey.

54

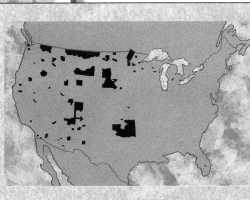

RESERVATION LANDS

The dark color marks the reservations set up by the United States government in the west. These small areas often had poor soil and a bad climate. Native Americans were expected to grow their own food, and this caused great hardship because many tribes had never farmed before. They were unable to hunt or to move around freely any more, and their new life often made them feel like prisoners.

COLORING CRAYONS

Some Native Americans who ran reservation stores could not write. They used crayons to draw pictures of what they sold.

SEWING LESSONS

In the reservation schools, children wore uniforms and were taught to read and write English. The girls used sewing machines to make European-style clothing.

COILED CLAY
Zuni craftspeople still use the traditional coil method for making pots out of local clays. They apply paints mixed from minerals with a chewed yucca leaf brush.

MICKEY MOCCASINS
Beadwork is a very old Native American craft. The designs of some moccasins now show modern influences.

Arts and Crafts

Native Americans made practical and beautifully crafted objects for everyday use. Their ceremonial clothing and sacred things were richly decorated. Painting, carving and embroidery told stories and were linked with the spirits through designs that had special meanings. Skills such as basketry, pottery and weaving have been passed down from one generation to another for many centuries. The Navajo learned silversmithing from the Mexicans in the 1850s, and then taught the Hopi and Zuni. Today, many artists and craftspeople use modern materials and tools. They take ideas from the twentieth century and blend them with patterns from the past, often using vibrant colors in their work. Native American arts and crafts are now famous throughout the world.

HANDCRAFTED JEWELRY
Turquoise, mined by Southwestern tribes, is the stone of happiness, health and good fortune.

FETISH BOWL
Southwestern tribes collected good luck objects called fetishes. They kept them in bowls painted with crushed turquoise. Some fetishes were strapped to the outside.

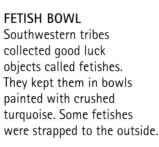

MINIATURE KACHINA

Some Zuni and Hopi artists make kachina dolls to sell. This one wears a mask topped with a feather plume and carries a rattle in its right hand.

WEAVERS OF THE SOUTHWEST

After the Navajo obtained sheep from Spanish colonists, they began to raise flocks successfully. The women learned to weave from their Pueblo neighbors and developed their own bold and colorful patterns. They made clothing from wool and from the cotton they planted, and traded woven goods with neighboring tribes throughout the Southwest. This blanket is more than 100 years old. It has warp threads of cotton and weft threads of wool. Today, Navajo weavers make heavier rugs for the floor and sell them to tourists.

PIECES OF SILVER

Navajo jewelers often make belts from sterling silver. This one has oval shell shapes alternating with butterfly spacers and is set with natural green turquoise stones.

CLAY FIGURE

"Uncle Fidel's Cousin San Luis" was sculptured by a Pueblo potter, Nora Naranjo-Morse. When Nora has her hands on clay, she feels she has "come home."

DID YOU KNOW?

The Zuni believed that the spirits of animals and plants lived in objects that looked like them. Traditional animal fetishes were usually naturally shaped stones. Modern ones may be carved.

Discover more in Totems, Masks and Kachinas

57

The Future

Native Americans suffered badly from the changes caused by European settlement. Many people died and some tribes disappeared altogether. Now, the number of Native Americans is growing as more healthy babies are born each year. Governments are beginning to recognize Native Americans' rights as citizens of the United States and Canada. More than half now live outside reservations. Today, Native Americans try to blend the old with the new and to keep their religious ceremonies, customs and languages alive. Cherokee schoolchildren learn to speak Cherokee and have lessons in Cherokee lifestyle. At powwows throughout the country, young children take part in social and competition dances, performing to the beat of the drums. They dress in tribal costumes and put on face paint for these happy celebrations.

STICK GAMES
Native Americans still play the old games of chance, and gamble with bunches of painted sticks.

SACRED CEREMONIAL CHAMBER
Pueblo villagers meet in the kivas to discuss local government, to train the young and to build altars and pray.

58

MOSAIC NECKLACE
This modern necklace was made from silver, inlaid with semi-precious stones and shells. It depicts the Zuni rainbow god.

ZUNI SACRED MOUNTAIN
Today's Native Americans visit their ancestral sacred sites for spiritual guidance. These places are holy ground where plants, paths, shrines and rocks all have religious meaning and must not be disturbed.

HOPI BASKETS
The Hopi method of making baskets has not changed for hundreds of years.

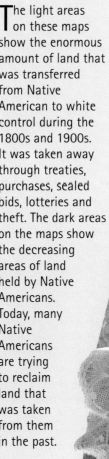

LOSS OF TRADITIONAL LANDS

1850

1865

1880

1995

The light areas on these maps show the enormous amount of land that was transferred from Native American to white control during the 1800s and 1900s. It was taken away through treaties, purchases, sealed bids, lotteries and theft. The dark areas on the maps show the decreasing areas of land held by Native Americans. Today, many Native Americans are trying to reclaim land that was taken from them in the past.

People and Events

Native Americans passed the stories of their people from one generation to the next by word of mouth. After European writing was introduced, a more permanent record was made of many of these traditions. Accounts were written of the chieftains who struggled with the white settlers for possession of their homelands. Other Native Americans made it into the history books as well. The following are a few of them.

Sequoyah

Sequoyah, who lived from about 1773 to 1843, had a Cherokee mother and an English father. He believed that white people had power because they could read and write, so he created a written version of the Cherokee language. There was a separate symbol for each of the 86 syllables.

Geronimo

The Apache chief Geronimo was born in 1829. He was first called "Goyanthlay", which means "One Who Yawns." When Mexican troops killed his family, he became a fierce warrior, feared by both Mexican and American soldiers. Geronimo eventually surrendered and in 1905 took part in President Theodore Roosevelt's presidential parade in Washington. He died in 1909.

Sitting Bull

Sitting Bull was a respected shaman and a Sioux chief. He led a group at the Battle of Little Bighorn but was too old to take an active part in the fighting. He fled to Canada with his people but later surrendered to United States troops. He was killed by reservation police in 1890.

Red Cloud

Red Cloud, war leader of the Oglala Sioux, counted 80 coups in his lifetime of fighting. He bargained with the government to keep some of the Great Plains for his people. In 1870 he said to officials: "Our nation is melting away like the snow on the sides of the hills where the sun is warm, while your people are like blades of grass in spring when the summer is coming."

"Custer's Last Stand"

In 1868, General George Armstrong Custer and his United States cavalry forces brutally attacked unarmed women and children in a Sioux village. On June 25, 1876, bands of Sioux and Cheyenne warriors trapped and killed Custer and his men at the Battle of Little Bighorn. It was the last major victory of Plains Indians against white soldiers.

Battle at Wounded Knee

In 1890, the United States army attacked unarmed Sioux at Wounded Knee. About 200 Sioux were shot and another 100 who escaped, froze to death in the hills. This was a terrible day in Native American history.

Navajo Code Talkers

The languages of several Native American tribes were used for coding messages in the Second World War. The Navajo code talkers developed terms to describe military movements and equipment: a submarine was an "iron fish;" a machine gun was a "fast shooter."

N. Scott Momaday

Native American author N. Scott Momaday won the Pulitzer Prize in 1969 for *House Made of Dawn*. The story is about Native American people in modern times.

Siege at Wounded Knee

In 1973, an armed band of representatives from the American Indian Movement occupied the village of Wounded Knee. They said the government had not listened to their requests for fairer treatment. After 71 days, officials from the government negotiated a withdrawal.

Native Americans were organized in different tribal groups, spread out across what is now Greenland, Canada and North America. The Sioux, who pitched their tepees on the Great Plains, were as different from the Tlingits on the Northwest Coast as people from Sweden are from those who live in Greece today.

Tribes spoke their own languages, had particular religious customs and laws, and were different in many other ways. The roles of men and women varied greatly from group to group. There has not been space to put every Native American tribe in this book. This map shows the location of the tribes that are featured in this book and gives an example of one type of dwelling for each region.

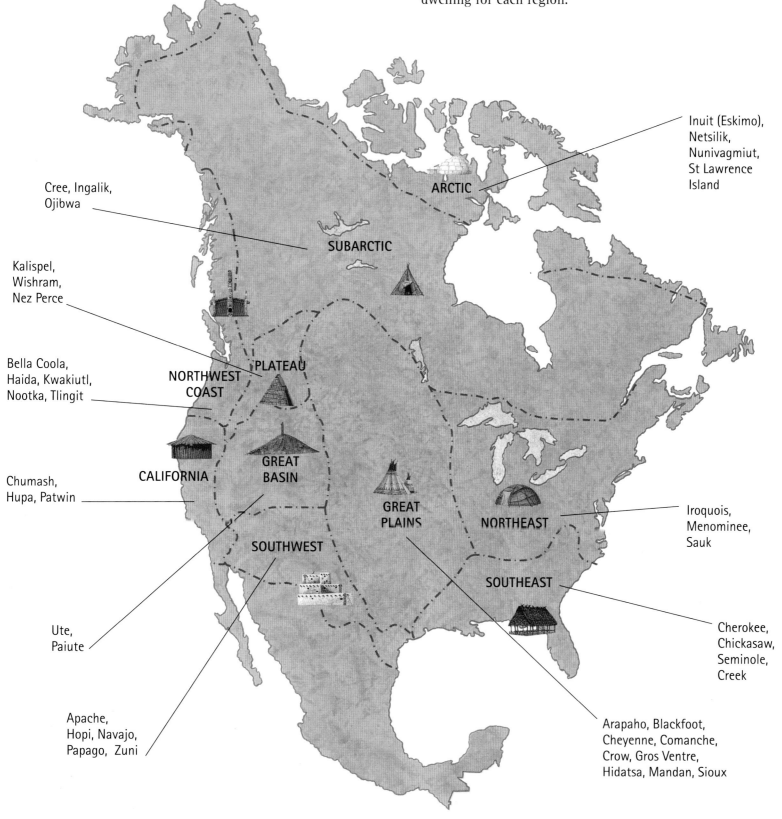

Cree, Ingalik, Ojibwa

Kalispel, Wishram, Nez Perce

Bella Coola, Haida, Kwakiutl, Nootka, Tlingit

Chumash, Hupa, Patwin

Ute, Paiute

Apache, Hopi, Navajo, Papago, Zuni

SUBARCTIC

ARCTIC

Inuit (Eskimo), Netsilik, Nunivagmiut, St Lawrence Island

PLATEAU

NORTHWEST COAST

CALIFORNIA

GREAT BASIN

SOUTHWEST

GREAT PLAINS

NORTHEAST

SOUTHEAST

Iroquois, Menominee, Sauk

Cherokee, Chickasaw, Seminole, Creek

Arapaho, Blackfoot, Cheyenne, Comanche, Crow, Gros Ventre, Hidatsa, Mandan, Sioux

61

Glossary

Thunderbird mask

Inuit grass socks

Rawhide playing cards

Inuit snow goggles

Saddle bag

ancestor A member of your family who died a long time ago.

archaeologist Someone who studies the cultures of the past using the things people left behind them as clues, for example, bones, tools, clothing and jewelry.

bow The front of a boat– pronounced to rhyme with "cow."

bow drill A tool used for drilling holes in bone and shell– bow is pronounced to rhyme with "no."

bullboat Circular craft made from a framework of willow branches covered with buffalo hide.

Cannibal Spirit An unfriendly spirit in the stories of the Northwest Coast Kwakiutl tribe.

cattail A tall marsh plant with reedlike leaves. Many Native Americans ate the pollen and roots.

chickee An open-sided dwelling, thatched with palm branches and raised above the ground on stilts. Used in swampy areas in the Southeast.

clan A group of people related to each other by ancestry or marriage.

coup A Plains warrior scored a coup when he touched his enemy with a coup stick (a long slender branch used in battle), lance or anything else held in the hand.

Coyote The mischievous wolf spirit that loved playing tricks.

creation stories Native Americans told different stories to explain where they came from.

dentalium shells The long, narrow, tubular shells of various burrowing seashore creatures. Also called tusk or tooth shells. Used for jewelry.

emblem A decorative mark or symbol that means something special.

ermine A type of stoat closely related to the weasel. Its white winter coat with black-tipped tail was prized for decorating ceremonial clothing.

Eskimo (see Inuit) Dwellers in the Arctic region. Eskimo means "eaters of raw meat," but they cooked at least part of their daily ration.

fetishes Natural objects, such as an unusually shaped stone, a perfect ear of corn or a shell.

The Southwestern tribes believed they brought supernatural power.

gauntlet glove A glove with a long cuff.

gourd The fruit of a species of plant that includes squashes. The dried shells were used as rattles and containers.

harpoon A wooden shaft with a detachable head tied to a long line. When a sea mammal was harpooned, the head stuck in the animal's flesh. Its attempts to escape were slowed by a drag float.

hogan A Navajo dwelling built of timber and poles covered with bark and dirt.

husky A breed of dog. They were the Inuits' (Eskimos') only domestic animal.

Ice Age A time when large parts of the Earth were covered with glaciers.

igloo A temporary winter dwelling built by some Arctic tribes from hard-packed snow.

Inuit (see Eskimo) Many tribes in the Arctic prefer to be known as Inuit. This is their word for "people."

kachinas Supernatural spirits who guided the tribes of the Southwest. For six months of the year, kachinas lived in the World Below and came up above ground from the winter solstice to the summer solstice.

kiva A place of worship and a council chamber, usually built below ground.

lean-to A framework of poles covered with branches and grasses to form a simple shelter.

loincloth Cloth or skin draped between the legs and looped through a belt. Worn by many Native Americans living in a warm climate.

mano A small stone used for crushing corn.

medicine man/woman A shaman with special powers to heal and contact the spirits.

metate A large stone slab used for grinding corn.

migrating When people or animals move from one country or place to another.

mythology (Native Americans) Stories passed down by word of mouth from one generation to another.

New World A name used by the Europeans for the land area that included Canada, North America and South America.

Old World The part of the world that was known by Europeans before the discovery of Canada and the Americas. It included Europe, Asia and Africa.

parfleche A saddlebag made from rawhide in the pattern of an envelope. This word comes from the French "parer une flèche," meaning "to turn an arrow."

porcupine An animal covered with long protective quills. Native American women softened and dyed the quills and used them for embroidery.

prow Another word for the bow of a boat.

puffin A diving bird with a brightly coloured beak. Arctic tribes ate them and used their beaks and feathers for decoration.

Raven A spirit worshipped by the Native Americans.

resin A thick, waterproof, sticky substance obtained from some plants and trees.

ritual The pattern of behavior for a ceremonial dance or religious ceremony.

sacred object Something used in a religious ceremony, for example, a buffalo's skull.

saguaro A giant desert cactus with a sweet red fruit.

Sea Grizzly Bear A spirit creature carved on masks and totem poles.

shaman A medicine man or woman with special powers to heal and contact the spirits.

sinew An animal tendon used by Native Americans as sewing thread.

Skywoman A character in Iroquois creation stories.

soapstone A variety of soft stone that could be easily worked with a knife or hand drill.

stern The back of a boat.

supernatural Relating to things belonging to the world of the spirits.

sweat lodge An airtight hut filled with steam—the Native American equivalent of a sauna.

swivel A part that kept the harness on a dog sled from becoming tangled.

symbol A decorative mark in a painting or carving that means something special.

tanning The process for turning animal skins into leather.

Thunderbird A spirit worshipped by the tribes of the Northwest Coast.

thwart A crosspiece inside a canoe that pushes out the sides and forms a seat for the people who row the boat.

travois A platform for baggage formed by poles, joined together by a web of ropes. It was tied to the back of a horse or a dog.

tule A species of cattail found in the lakes and marshes of western America.

tule pollen Fine, powdery yellow grains produced by cattail flowers as they turn to seed.

tundra A treeless area with permanently frozen subsoil that lies between the ice of the Arctic and the timber line of North America and Eurasia.

umiak A rowing boat made from whalebone covered with walrus hide and waterproofed with seal oil. It had a single sail and was used by the Inuit to hunt whales.

vision A religious experience that brought a person into contact with the spirits.

vision quest An expedition made alone in order to see a vision. Boys went on their first quest at puberty to test their courage. They sometimes stayed for days in an isolated place without food.

wampum White and purple disc-shaped beads made from shells. Native Americans exchanged them as ceremonial gifts. Wampum began to have monetary value after the Europeans arrived.

wickiup A dwelling used in the Southwest made of poles covered with branches.

wigwam A shelter used by tribes in the Northeast and Great Lakes. They bent four saplings towards a center and covered them with long strips of bark sewn together.

woolly mammoth A large hairy animal that became extinct at the end of the Ice Age. It had a trunk like an elephant and curved tusks.

yucca A native plant— the chewed stem made an excellent paintbrush.

War shield

Net gauge

Apache basket

Tepee ornaments

Navajo blanket

Index